¡Vamos al Zoo!

por Kari Capone
ilustrado por Chow Su

Scott Foresman
is an imprint of

Glenview, Illinois • Boston, Massachusetts • Chandler, Arizona
Upper Saddle River, New Jersey

Every effort has been made to secure permission and provide appropriate credit for photographic material. The publisher deeply regrets any omission and pledges to correct errors called to its attention in subsequent editions.

Unless otherwise acknowledged, all photographs are the property of Pearson.

Photo locations denoted as follows: Top (T), Center (C), Bottom (B), Left (L), Right (R), Background (Bkgd)

Illustrations by Chow Su

Photograph 8 Peter Anderson/©DK Images

ISBN 13: 978-0-328-53300-8
ISBN 10:   0-328-53300-9

Copyright © by Pearson Education, Inc., or its affiliates. All rights reserved. Printed in the United States of America. This publication is protected by copyright, and permission should be obtained from the publisher prior to any prohibited reproduction, storage in a retrieval system, or transmission in any form or by any means, electronic, mechanical, photocopying, recording, or likewise. For information regarding permissions, write to Pearson Curriculum Rights & Permissions, One Lake Street, Upper Saddle River, New Jersey 07458.

Pearson® is a trademark, in the U.S. and/or other countries, of Pearson plc or its affiliates.

Scott Foresman® is a trademark, in the U.S. and/or other countries, of Pearson Education, Inc., or its affiliates.

2 3 4 5 6 7 8 9 10 V0N4 13 12 11 10

¡Vamos a ver los monos!

Muy bien, Rubén.

Luego veremos las focas.

¡Vamos a ver las focas!
Mira, ésa puede balancear el balón.

¡Vamos a ver las cabras!
Mira, ésa quiere comer
una ramita.

¡Vamos a ver los osos!
Mira, los bebés duermen.

Mira, qué altas son las jirafas.

Rubén, es tarde.

¡Adiós, jirafas bonitas!

Las jirafas

Leamos juntos

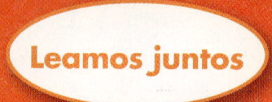

Las jirafas pueden medir hasta 19 pies de alto y pesar más de 4,000 libras. El cuello de una jirafa mide unos ocho pies de largo. Cuando nace, una jirafita puede medir ¡seis pies de alto!

Las jirafas resisten más tiempo sin beber agua que un camello. Cuando beben, pueden tomar hasta 12 galones de agua de una vez.

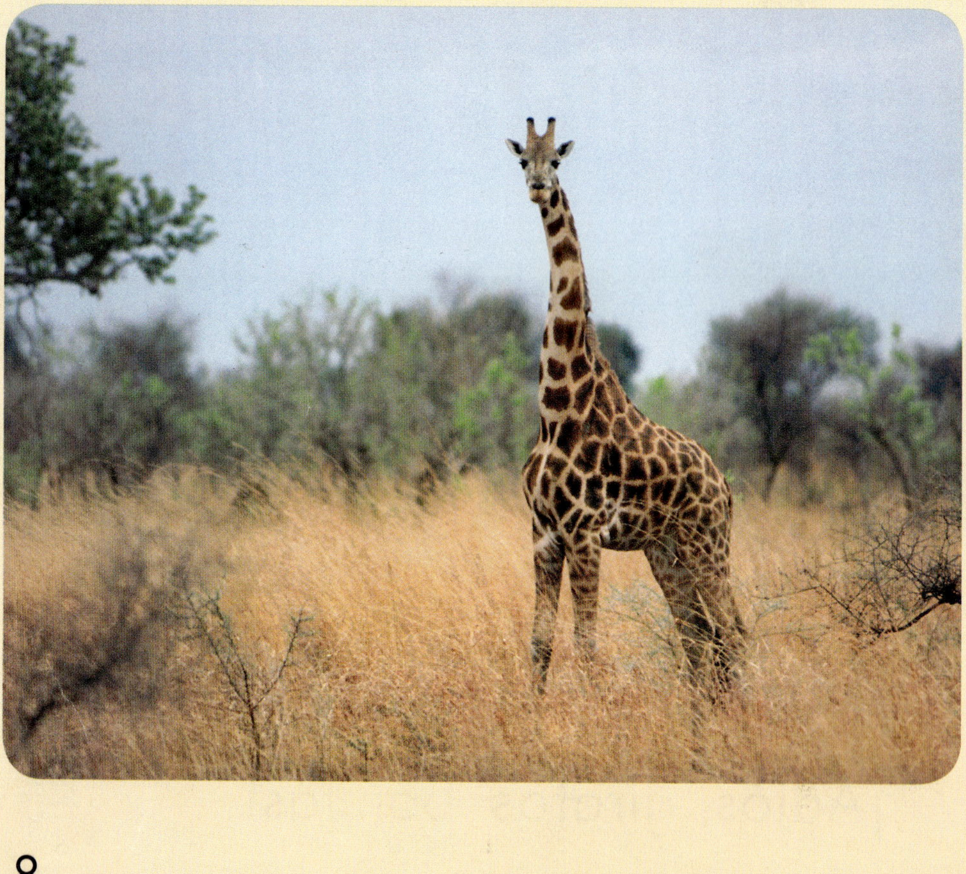